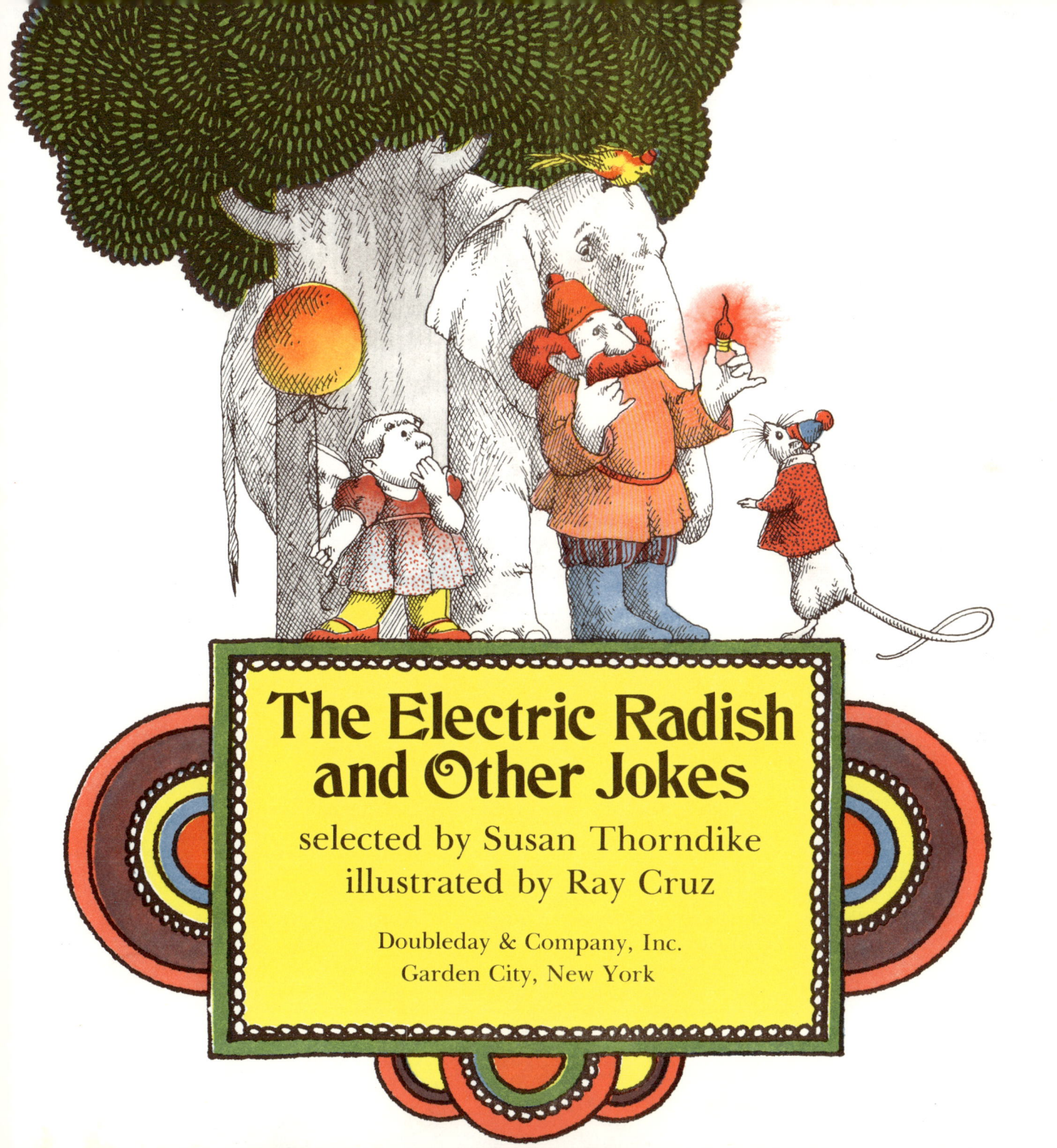

The Electric Radish and Other Jokes

selected by Susan Thorndike
illustrated by Ray Cruz

Doubleday & Company, Inc.
Garden City, New York

Illustrations © 1973 by Ray Cruz
All Rights Reserved
Printed in the United States of America

What is red, has a tail, and hums?

An electric radish.

What does a 500-pound mouse say to a cat?

Here, kitty, kitty, kitty.

A woman who wanted cannons to look pretty.

Mother Kangaroo: Oh no! I've had my pocket picked!

Boy: None, but I want to grow some.

Mother tiger to baby tiger: What are you doing?
Baby tiger: I'm chasing a hunter around a tree.

What goes 999 thump, 999 thump, 999 thump?

A centipede with a wooden leg.

A lost camel.

Because they have two left feet.

How does a hippopotamus get down from a tree?

He sits on a leaf
and waits for the fall.

How does a monster count to 17?

On his fingers.

Why did the elephant paint his toenails red?

So he could hide in the strawberry patch.

Sit in a tree and act like a nut.

Because his powder puff is on the wrong end.

Climbs on an acorn and waits.

Cheer him up.

Frankie: An elephant hanging over a cliff with his tail tied to a buttercup

If you had all those jokes told about you, you wouldn't want to be recognized either.

What **is yell**ow and green and eats grass?
A yellow and green grass-eater.

What is yellow and blue and eats grass?
A yellow and blue grass-eater?

Susan Thorndike received her B.A. in English and American literature from Brandeis University and prepared THE ELECTRIC RADISH AND OTHER JOKES while working at Doubleday & Company in the children's book department. She lives in New York City and in her spare time is learning to make pottery.

Ray Cruz, a native New Yorker, attended the High School of Art and Design, Pratt Institute, and Cooper Union and has been drawing all his life. He has illustrated a number of books, including THE STORYBOOK COOKBOOK, HORRIBLE HEPZIBAH, MARVELOUS MACHINES, and GREAT QUILLOW. Mr Cruz lives in Greenwich Village.